The House with Nine Oaks

Cultivating Strength for Your Family

ANGELA PHELPS

To My Family

Contents

Introduction

Since many people detour the introduction of a book, I will be brief.

Once upon a time, there was a family of nine...
blah, blah, blah...
and they lived happily ever after.
THE END

Well, maybe not *that* brief.

This book is an earnest endeavor, not to sketch a fairy-tale family or a reality-TV show clan, but rather to give form to the "blah, blah, blah." What does family life look like between the ellipsis points? All things considered, there is much that happens in a family – day by day and year by year – mundane and monumental.

The title of this book uses the theme of oak trees, nine to be exact. Oaks are known for their strength. Families can also be known for their strength when life is lived with purpose and principle.

However, before you despair that you have spent money on some how-to book with seven steps to a highly functional family, take heart and read on. I actually have something to share about family life that provides the words, sentences, and paragraphs in a story that is more than just "once upon a time."

Won't you join me?

"…In their righteousness, they will be like great oaks
that the Lord has planted for His own glory."
(Isaiah 61:3, NLT)

"…They will be called oaks of righteousness, a planting
of the Lord for the display of His splendor."
(Isaiah 61:3, NIV)

The Portrait of a Family

When I was a child, I was enamored by the portraits of stately families – the more regal the better. The father and mother would usually be seated in ornate chairs with the children placed around them, all of them dressed elegantly; sometimes the family dog even made it into the scene. I would imagine their home; surely they had a life of ease with the best of everything. I was also sure the parents were loving and kind and the children were always well-behaved, never bickering among themselves. (I am not sure on what planet or quantum realm such perfection of humanity would actually exist, but as children, we imagine amazing things.)

Something happened in my heart any time I looked at these types of pictures; an ideal was formed. I wanted to grow up and have a family like that, full of love and wealth and every good thing. Such desires did not spring from some psychologically-warped childhood that was lacking in the basic necessities of life. I grew up in a home where I always felt loved and cared for, even by extended family. (What a blessing!) Perhaps I just wanted to go a step further.

When I began my own family, I truly wanted to do things right. I believed that if I could succeed in this venture, I would send my children into adulthood with a good conscience toward God, a love for others, and a passion for their country.

What would it take to succeed in this venture? This was the million-dollar question. I came to understand that there were actually some pillars in this architecture of a happy home, such as wisdom, diligence, love, and laughter. There were boundaries to set up, training to be initiated, and correction to be given along with lots of love to be shared and lots of fun to be enjoyed. There was much planting to be done in the spring of young lives so that a harvest would come in the autumn of adulthood.

To become the family in the photo, there would have to be the purchase of ornate chairs and elegant clothing. Fold-out lawn chairs and clearance-rack bargains just would not do. The dog would need to be a sleek purebred rather than a mutt that wandered into the neighborhood. The house would need to be a sprawling estate rather than a remodeled foreclosure.

And the family…well, who knows if my family will ever pose for a grand painting or exquisite photograph? We may never be seen as those who are stately, but I have kept in my heart and mind the portrait of a family who chooses a noble life: pleasing God, loving others, and embracing country.

The First Oak – Peace

A still pond, a pastoral painting, a gentle lullaby – these all emulate the feeling of peace. At first glance, we may think peaceful elements are fragile, and yet there is a strength of peace that seems foundational.

As we begin this story of family, peacefulness is what attracted me to my husband Randal. He was a fun-loving person, easy to get along with. He always seemed to be at peace with himself and others. Not that I was a raging storm, but he was able (on more than one occasion) to calm a stormy situation in my soul. I believe that my husband's peace laid a foundation for our relationship, then for our marriage, and ultimately, for our family.

With this in mind, **the first oak among our nine is Peace.** Let me say that a peaceful home is worth attaining; it is worth our efforts. The goal of peace is not merely some soulish endeavor of bringing quiet to chaos; it is a biblical plan of bringing the ways of God's Kingdom right into our homes. Here is what God says about it:

> "My people will dwell in a peaceful habitation, in secure dwellings, and in quiet resting places…"
> (Isaiah 32:18, NKJV)

Regardless of the level of activity, one's home should be a restful place for the heart. In our years before children, a calm moment did not seem difficult to find. Other than occasional church activities or family gatherings, we spent our evenings together; but as the children arrived, evening hours brought a few more challenges. Dinner had to be on the table at the right time, toys needed to be picked up (at least in the living area), baths and bedtime, and maybe even the appearance of an adoring wife.

Perhaps it was during these years when I made the association of the cleaned-up living area with creating a peaceful atmosphere and honoring others. Since my husband's work hours were set, he usually arrived home at the same time each evening. Knowing this, I would have the children pick up their toys and books in our living area a few minutes before his arrival. Many were the evenings when Randal walked in the door and gave us this compliment, "Wow! This place looks great!"

I believe the clearing away of the day's clutter honored the head of our household and gave an outward appearance of peace: a place for everything, and everything in its place. (By "clearing away," I do not mean cleaning. We did not dust, vacuum, etc.; we just picked up toys and straightened the room. Cleaning was done on another day.) Beyond the daily application which affected our family, we made sure that when visitors arrived, they were able to enjoy a peaceful environment with no clutter, no television competing for our attention, and no misbehaving children. Over the years, the prevailing compliment to our family has been regarding the atmosphere in our home.

Lest you think each moment at our house has been as smooth as silk, please be aware that I believe peace is worked for, achieved, attained. While there are phlegmatic personalities and tranquil settings which seem to naturally exude peace, the "peaceable fruit of righteousness" (Hebrews 12:11) is just that; it is fruit, growth from a life source. Grapes are the fruit of grapevines; apples are the fruit of apple trees. In this case, "the work of righteousness shall be peace" (Isaiah 32:17). In the same way that trees and plants grow fruit and flowers, doing things in a right way, even in a righteous way, yields the fruit or evidence of peacefulness.

A flavorful meal does not just happen; it is the result of some time preparing and cooking. A well-manicured lawn does not just happen; it is the result of time spent pushing a mower and pulling some weeds. A peaceful home does not just happen; it is the result of choosing and doing right things.

What are some "right things" to do in our families? Say encouraging things to one another, have meals together (with the television off), keep the bills paid, the house clean, the lawn mowed, the car running. Whole books have been written on any of these topics and much more; but the bottom line is to *value one another*. When we do these things while keeping others in mind, there is a lot more purpose, a lot more reward, and there is a lot more peace.

Surely we have all experienced the disruptions that invade our family when we do not stay caught up on something as simple as laundry. Not having clean underwear or t-shirts can get really personal. I have felt a pang of compassion for the kids when I got behind on laundry and they needed clean socks. When everything is in its place, the general sense of angst or tears of frustration is absent; there is peace.

Years ago, I became frustrated about my weekly grocery process. It went something like this: 1) make the weekly menu, 2) make the weekly grocery list, then of course 3) actually go to the store and do the shopping. I would sit down and stare at a blank piece of paper, trying to think of meals. Then, one day I wrote out a list of favorite meals. This was helpful, but it seemed as if the cycle was not long enough; I needed more meals to go with all the other days of the month. Then, I sat down and made out a menu for a whole month, only duplicating one meal (the Sunday roast). Wow! I felt like I had summited Mt. Everest!

Just this simple act of creating a menu caused a better flow when it came to a very important part of our household: eating. Now I know there are processes for using coupons or even cooking for a month at a time, but this book is about telling what has worked for our family and encouraging you to find out what will work for yours. The point is to keep the process in a fluid movement so you or your kids are not standing in front of the pantry or refrigerator every afternoon, wondering what is for snack or dinner.

We can certainly make a religion out of any system (meals, laundry, lawn work). Even if you find a process that works for you and your family, it will probably change at some point. All nine of us used to sit down to dinner every evening; however, our kids grew up, began working and having their own social schedules, then they moved away from home. Things change. The important thing is to find and do what works for the season of life we find ourselves living.

Beyond the practical moments of life, there are spiritual and soulish aspects that matter. One thing that quiets the drama of life is keeping God first in the family. One of the ways we do that is praying together. When I speak of praying, I mean several things: 1) praying in an on-going manner, such as at mealtimes or every night before bed with children and as a couple, 2) praying when moments of crisis arise, such as sickness, accidents, news of tragedy, and 3) praying when "mountains" need to move (Mark 11:22-26), such as long-standing situations of relational conflict, unhealthy behavior, or illness.

Especially for children, a prayer can calm their fast-beating heart after a fall or an accident. When our children were young, prayer and a hug always came after the bandage, and it settled them. Even after times of discipline, we prayed with them to set things right between us and the Lord. Also, prayer before bedtime was always a common practice for us, bringing what felt like the proper close to the day, like the words THE END at the finish of a story.

For our marriage, a monumental moment came when Randal and I realized peace could be achieved by the power of agreement. Here is where we saw it:

"Again I say to you that if two of you agree on earth concerning anything that they ask, it will be done for them by My Father in heaven."
(Matthew 18:19, NKJV)

Two people coming from different families present the opportunity for selfishness, fussing, strife, or even down-right domestic war, yet choosing to live in agreement will literally keep our families together. Preservation of the human family unit at its most shallow point may just be to bring all of us some form of happiness. Children can say, "My daddy and mommy still love each other, still live together." Couples can say, "We are not part of some negative statistic." All of this could give us a warm, fuzzy feeling inside, which is not altogether bad. However, what if we choose peace rather than strife, knowing the end result will preserve our family, the very model for community?

We have probably all heard the phrase about when two people think the same, one of them is not needed; yet look at these scriptural admonitions to be "like-minded":

"…fulfill my joy, by being like-minded, having the same love, being of one accord, of one mind."
(Philippians 2:2, NKJV)

"Nevertheless, to the degree that we have already attained, let us walk by the same rule, let us be of the same mind."
(Philippians 3:16, NKJV)

"Finally, all of you be of one mind, having compassion for one another; love as brothers, be tenderhearted, be courteous…"
(1 Peter 3:8, NKJV)

"Now may the God of patience and comfort grant you to be like-minded toward one another according to Christ Jesus, that you may with one mind and one mouth glorify the God and Father of our Lord Jesus Christ."
(Romans 15:5, 6, NKJV)

Randal and I purposed that we would choose agreement, not just agreeing to disagree, but we would really find common ground. Our marriage became stronger because of it. When a couple decides to agree with one another, the outcome is powerful, for good or for evil. The New Testament couple Aquila and Priscilla seemed to be models of agreeing for good as they spread the Gospel message and mentored believers (Acts 18:2, 18, 26), but Ananias and Sapphira literally died (Acts 5) because they agreed to carry out an evil plan. (Remember Bonnie and Clyde?)

Here is another verse that has shaped our marriage for peace:

"Can two walk together, unless they're agreed?"
(Amos 3:3, NKJV)

Sometimes when I hear this verse, the picture of a three-legged race comes to mind. The success of crossing the finish line will not be realized if the two participants do not "agree" and run together. When all the parts of a machine work together, the result is motion; when all the instruments of a symphony play together, the result is harmony. Strife clogs the workings of a family's well-oiled machine; it brings dissonance to its melody. This is why agreement must be a priority to achieve peace.

The stance of unison also aided our parenting skills so our children could not manipulate situations; they came to fully understand that Dad and Mom would talk about their requests or behavior, then we would give them a unified answer. Randal was so good at this. Whenever one of the kids would ask him if they could do a certain thing or have a certain thing, he would ask them, "What did your mom say?" After their response, he would say, "I'll talk with her and then let you know." They knew they should always tell the truth or the desired objective would not be attained.

On another note, I believe that one of the foremost ways of keeping peace between a husband and wife is Have Sex Often. The satisfaction of an intimate moment seems to work wonders in keeping a couple happy and at peace with one another. In a marriage where fidelity is valued, we need to fulfill one another's desire for intimacy and not leave the one we care for stranded in some place of longing or loneliness.

Additionally, choosing to be romantic with our spouse affirms the feeling of being *chosen* all over again. While we do not solely live by our emotions, the fact that we fell in love before we married (or somewhere along the way) reminds us of how special it is to be chosen. Out of all the women on the planet, my husband asked me to be with him for life; and out of all the men on the planet, I chose to say, "Yes, I'll spend the rest of my life with you."

This idea of being chosen by our spouse seriously trumps the elementary schoolyard "warm fuzzies" of being chosen for a team at recess. Being chosen can be affirmed by romantic gestures of thoughtfulness and flirtation, which go a long way in aiding our peacefulness as a couple. Have a date night, bring her flowers, make his favorite meal, go to a movie together, leave a card and the favorite candy bar on his/her pillow. Think about it, and you will get ideas that will inspire. Most of all, sex for a married couple is our opportunity to continue reminding our beloved that we belong to and love one another, body and soul.

With this in mind, a couple's concord is even like a shield when interacting with friends and family. The sound of harmony can seemingly become a weapon, stilling any plan others might have to divide and conquer.

Here is a simple poem I wrote years ago as I was thinking about this concept:

As trite as it seems,
Two can be one.
In action and thought,
A battle is won.

Strife cannot stay!
It cannot remain!
Agreement in love
Is victory attained.

When we face the enemies of peace – things like chaos, anger, disarray, or even confusion – as a family or on a personal level, we need to let peace act as an umpire, calling the plays of our life. Counsel from others is good, but someone else cannot tell us which job to take, who to marry, or where to live. Following the peace that is inside us helps make things clear. When there is a *scratchy* feeling in our heart about the things with which we are involved, we need to re-evaluate. A pendulum swing is not always the answer; sometimes we only have to make a small adjustment.

At whatever stage we find ourselves on this family trek, we can and should choose a peaceful journey. All of us – husbands, wives, fathers, mothers, children, or siblings – must take to heart that peace is a powerful element in our lives.

When Jesus calmed the storm, He said, "Peace, be still" (Mark 4:39). And as we live from day to day, facing the storms of life or the dishes in the sink, strength will come as we "let the peace of God rule..." in our hearts (Colossians 3:15 AMPC).

STRENGTHEN YOUR ROOTS

*Choose peace for your family; begin with making a decision that no one will keep you from having a peaceful home and loving relationships.

*Take a moment to get a plan for simple processes in your home, such as making a menu for the week or the month, planning and doing the duties of your home.

*Do something romantic for your spouse this week.

The Second Oak – Truth

When we think of a courtroom witness raising his hand and swearing to "tell the truth, the whole truth, and nothing but the truth," it is a sobering thought. However, for a system of law to be just, truth must be upheld. Likewise, for a marriage to be sound, truth must be valued, and for a family to be healthy, truth must be practiced. With these thoughts, allow me to share with you **the second oak among our nine: Truth.**

I see the principle of truth to be as clean as my grandmother's laundry flapping in the breeze or a fresh-fallen snow or a mountain brook. With synonyms such as honesty and accuracy, why would we *not* want to embrace truth? Perhaps because it can also be a two-edged sword; we welcome its certainty but sometimes fear its effects.

Truth can be as simple as understanding that two plus two is four, or truth can be astonishing. Remember these astonishing movie moments? Luke Skywalker found out that Darth Vader was his father. Mary Jane found out Peter Parker was Spiderman. How about these astonishing, real-life moments? The United States found out that unfriendly missiles were as close as Cuba. U.S. citizens found out airplanes were being used as weapons of terrorism.

I became aware of the deepest truth when I was just six years old. By *the deepest truth*, I mean the understanding that God my Heavenly Father loved me so much He gave His only Son Jesus to be the sacrifice for my sins. What sins could a six-year-old have done? Probably not many, but because I am human, I needed a Savior. Whether we are six or sixty, we all need a Savior.

"…for all have sinned and fall short of the glory of God…"
(Romans 3:23, NKJV)

"For God so loved the world that He gave His only begotten Son, that whoever believes in Him should not perish but have everlasting life."
(John 3:16, NKJV)

My simple conversion moment happened in what we church-goers call *children's church* (like an adult church service but for children). At my church in Grand Prairie, Texas, children's church was led by a tall, older woman named Serene. She had jet-black hair that was always wound tight and placed in a bun on her head. Her demeanor was bubbly, and she loved to sing and clap; but most of all, she loved to tell kids Bible stories and talk about Jesus.

On a particular Sunday as she talked about Jesus, I had a light-bulb moment that so many before me have had: I needed a Savior. So I did it; I asked Jesus to forgive me of my sins and be my Savior. I suppose the experience was as glorious as it gets for a six-year-old; at least I can say that my heart was flooded with joy and peace. (If you would like to pray a similar prayer to receive Jesus as your Savior, please see the back of this book.)

Later, when I was in high school, my English class took a test. Before we began, the teacher gave us a warning: if she saw any cheating, she would give the student a zero. During the test, a popular student leaned over and asked me for an answer. I was torn about what to do. Do I give him the answer and get a zero or keep to myself and be known as a do-gooder? I gave the answer, but I felt so guilty that I told the teacher at the end of class. She said she had seen me do it and was very disappointed; however, she was very merciful in not giving me a zero. I had studied, and I was ready for the test; the other student was not ready for it. This became such a deciding moment for me. Within the next couple months, two other students asked me for test answers. Confidently, I did not give the answers and felt no shame.

Now for some, life might not be as sweet as a six-year-old girl who asks Jesus to be her Savior or a high school student who wants to do the right thing. There are always those in the crowd who scorn the truth, who prefer to tell a lie or to live a lie. Scripture speaks of those who resist the truth (2 Timothy 3:8) or who turn their ears away from the truth (2 Timothy 4:4). Even culture tries its hand at manipulating long-held principles into half-true statements, proving that "fables and commandments of men" can "turn us" from the truth (Titus 1:14).

With this in mind, I am especially appreciative that my parents embraced the truth taught in the Bible, and they raised my siblings and me to be truthful. Randal's parents also taught their family the same love of the truth, which makes it easy to see why Randal and I agreed on its importance.

When Randal and I were dating, we practiced being honest with one another; we did not play emotional or mental games in an effort to be manipulative. Early in our relationship, I remember being saucy to Randal about something. He looked me in the eye and said, "We're not going to play games," and he meant emotional, manipulative games. From that moment on, we did not. Because of this, I believe that truth was a strong guideline for trust in our relationship. Then as children were added to our family, we did not do a lot of teasing, because we always wanted our children to believe every word we said. We believed that too much jesting or too many pranks would lead our children to wonder what to believe, which was often what we saw modeled in other families. We certainly laughed together but not *at the expense* of each other.

In Christian circles, we have heard the Bible connected or synonymous with the truth. In Jesus' famous John 17 prayer to the Heavenly Father, He said, "...Your word is truth." With this in mind, we have always considered the Bible to be the foundation for our thoughts, actions, and beliefs. In an effort to pass this legacy of truth to our children, I often read the Bible to them, usually at nap time and bed time – just a couple of chapters but still enough for them to hear the stories and principles that make the Bible the strong standard that it still is. Reading the Bible for myself is a joy; reading the Bible to my kids opened many opportunities for conversation about attitudes and actions.

Beyond reading the Bible, I also believe we need to be sure the things we say are congruent with what the Bible teaches. Second Corinthians 4:13 says, "And since we have the same spirit of faith, according to what is written, 'I believed and therefore I spoke,' we also believe and therefore speak." Here are some things I have spoken over the years concerning our family:

*We are the redeemed of the Lord, and we say so.
(Psalm 107:2)
*Greater is He that is in us than he that is in the world.
(1 John 4:4)
*We are healed with the stripes of Jesus.
(Isaiah 53:5; 1 Peter 2:24)
*We prosper and we are in health, even as our soul prospers.
(3 John 2)
*Great is the peace of our children for they are taught of the Lord. (Isaiah 54:13)
*God supplies all our need according to His riches in glory.
(Philippians 4:19)

Our words have much power; they can ensnare us (Proverbs 6:2; 12:13, 14) or edify us (Proverbs 16:24; Ephesians 4:15). Our words can get us into or out of trouble (Proverbs 21:23). When it came to our family relationships, Randal and I were very watchful to say good things to one another and to our children, because we have always believed that to hear someone say they love us affirms our relationship as a husband, wife, son, or daughter. To hear someone compliment a quality in our life strengthens our very identity. To hear someone declare that we did a good job nurtures our desire to continue doing a good job.

While there is much benefit in speaking healthy words, we can also harm one another with our words. Contrary to television culture, family life is not about sitting around the house, seeing who can spit out the funniest or most cutting one-liners. Calling our spouse or child negative names will most likely have a lasting effect, and crafting words that sting will most likely produce their design. Also, we must keep in mind that offensive words will find their way back in some form of personal insult. Get rid of negative talk to yourself and to those around you, then you will be able to carry out this biblical command: "Let no corrupt word proceed out of your mouth, but what is good for necessary edification, that it may impart grace to the hearers" (Ephesians 4:29).

I believe we should ask ourselves what standard is guiding our thoughts and actions. As a Christian believer, are we guided by the Bible? As an American citizen, do we embrace the structure of the Constitution? As an employee, are we upholding the policies of our employer? As a student, are we compliant with our school guidelines or class syllabus? I am certainly not saying we should lazily saunter toward *any* standard just for the sake of being compliant, but rather I am suggesting that we evaluate the principles governing our lives.

The enemies of truth – lies, deception, or even half-truths – will always try to present a convincing argument; however, I believe truth is like a compass, leading us in the right direction. Truth is an anchor, holding us steady when the tides of life could cause us to drift. Truth is a cornerstone, causing the other elements of our life's building to align.

Standing in a courtroom with our hand raised is not the only time that life demands the truth to be our guide. Each day, our family, friends, and colleagues see us making choices that support the truth or deny it. What is the North Star that we follow? Let it be Truth!

STRENGTHEN YOUR ROOTS

*Choose to embrace a truthful lifestyle. Start by receiving *the deepest Truth* into your life; ask Jesus to be your Savior (See the back of this book if you would like a prayer for salvation).

*Value yourself and others by no longer telling half-truths or white lies.

*Let positive words change the atmosphere of your life and your home; no more negative talk.

*Read the Bible for yourself and to your children. There are Bibles and apps with daily reading plans to help us be diligent, or listen to the Bible while you drive, clean the house, or work in the garden.

*Find and attend a church that believes and preaches the truths of the Bible.

The Third Oak – Diligence

The famous inventor and statesman Benjamin Franklin once said, "Little strokes fell great oaks." In plain verbiage, keep chopping at a big tree, and it will finally come down. In figurative language, a diligent effort obtains a great reward. Think of the sculptor whose perseverance created the masterpiece *Winged Victory*, the artist who transformed the ceiling of the Sistine Chapel, the builders who raised towering structures from the ground, the inventor who gave us something as common and necessary as the light bulb. None of these accomplishments happened overnight. Perhaps we can think of the efforts of instructors who, over years of time, teach children to read *cat* then *category* then *catastrophe* or to learn mathematical concepts from simple addition to the complexities of calculus and beyond.

Diligence is attentiveness to an application; it is perseverance toward a particular labor, constancy to an activity. Diligence in our family relationships is the necessary dedication that makes a house a home. This is how we find ourselves at **the third oak among our nine: Diligence.**

One of the best ways I can think of beginning this topic is by mentioning the commitment it takes to nurture a baby. The pregnancy care and birthing of the child are only the beginning. A baby must be fed every couple of hours; its diaper must be changed often. It must sleep soundly, be held and loved. All of these activities are done hour after hour, day after day, week after week, month after month, and even year after year. (Consider a parent-directed lifestyle for your baby's and child's schedules; it is a diligent way to raise your child, and it makes an amazing difference.)

In my introduction of this book, I spoke of "mundane and monumental." Diligence is the resolve to do the mundane, knowing its every effort will have monumental reward. Each time we are diligent to keep our marriage vibrant, our children nurtured, our house orderly, our bills current, we ultimately will witness the mundane and common become the monumental and outstanding.

Merely saying the word *diligence* sounds noble but also a little boring. While *perseverance* does not have the same implication as *party*, the dinner must still be cooked, the lawn must be mowed, the trash must be removed, and the homework must be completed. I am sure there have been books written about turning the monotonous into the entertaining; however, this chapter is more along the lines of seeing the big picture and realizing what little – and sometimes dull – details must be done to bring about the desired result.

One day when my children were young, a woman asked me how my children were "so good." Before I thought of a clever answer, a simple one came flying out of my mouth. I said, "I think it's just being diligent to teach them the right things." She laughed at my reply and said it surely had to be something more than that. I was almost offended. It seemed ironic that she was complimenting the goodness of my children yet denying the validity of my answer. Surely *I* would be the one who knew how *my* kids had arrived at this moment in time in their present condition. They did not just wake up one morning in a state of goodness; they were loved and disciplined into this moment.

Additionally, we will not just wake up one morning "in love" with our spouse; we have to love and honor one another every day. We will not just wake up one morning smart; we have to study consistently. We will not just wake up one morning with a sparkling house; we have to clean it often. We will not just wake up one morning with a great credit score; we have to pay our bills regularly.

Years ago, our daily schedule looked something like this:

-Eat breakfast
-Get dressed, brush teeth, make beds
-Begin home schooling
-Break for mid-morning snack and play
-Continue schooling
-Break for lunch and play
-Back to schooling, finish early afternoon
-Playtime
-Afternoon chores
-More play
-Begin dinner, straighten the living area
-Randal home, dinner
-Playtime or evening activities
-Baths
-Read the Bible/pray, brush teeth, bedtime

We added laughter, hugs, picnics, and songs along the way.

We did this Monday through Thursday. Then on Friday, we cleaned house and washed our van. Randal and the boys did yard work on Saturday, and I usually bought groceries. Saturday night was about getting ready for church on Sunday morning: baths, clothes ironed and ready (along with hair bows, belts, socks and shoes), diaper bag prepared, etc. We wanted Sunday morning to be as easy as possible. Then, we went to church on Sunday, every Sunday.

When we cleaned house on Fridays, each child had his/her designated tasks, including changing the sheets, cleaning the bathroom, vacuuming, etc. I was given a book when my children were young that was invaluable; it listed age-appropriate chores, and I followed it very closely. As always, the training was the hardest part; but once the children learned, they were able to continue the work. For example, a child as young as two or three can fold washcloths, and they always thought it was fun. The older ones can learn to cook and trim the hedges, as well as do automobile tune-ups and gain financial understanding. Our kids even learned how to file their own taxes as teens.

Helping around our house with weekly duties was not an activity that came with compensation. One thing Randal and I taught our children was that you do not get paid to live. We all dirty the dishes, and we all take our turn washing them. We all sleep in a bed, and we all change our own sheets, clean the bathrooms we use, take out the trash, etc. Wise is the parent that teaches his/her child age-appropriate responsibilities.

These were our activities and schedules "years ago," and now our grown children have their own homes. Hopefully, the things they have learned will continue to guide them.

Diligent activity is not just limited to the things we can see; it is also important for our spirit and soul. Here are a few scriptures that make this point:

"...take heed to yourself, and diligently keep yourself, lest you forget the things your eyes have seen, and lest they depart from your heart all the days of your life. And teach them to your children and your grandchildren..."
(Deuteronomy 4:9, NKJV)

"Keep your heart with all diligence, for out of it spring the issues of life."
(Proverbs 4:23, NKJV)

"But without faith it is impossible to please Him [God], for he who comes to God must believe that He is, and that He is a rewarder of those who diligently seek Him."
(Hebrews 11:6, NKJV)

God knew that life must be lived in a consistent way. There were some things to be done every day, every week, every month, every year. That is why He said to "take heed to yourself." He knew the level of our diligence in life affects not only ourselves but also our children and even our grandchildren. It was a matter of legacy. It is still a matter of legacy.

I had the very enjoyable experience of living close to one set of my grandparents; they practically lived next door. We attended the same church, so whether it was Sunday morning, Sunday night, or Wednesday night, my siblings and I often asked if we could ride to church with them. Much to our delight, the answer was almost always "yes." Extremely rare was the moment when they did not attend services, and their constancy spoke volumes to others and to their children and grandchildren.

Consistent church attendance was not all they did. My grandmother taught a children's Sunday school class for years, and I remember them driving to pick up elderly members of the congregation, especially in the winter. My grandfather spent time every day at their kitchen table reading his Bible and writing down his thoughts on what he believed it meant. They also owned a small business which at times called on them to be benevolent to their patrons. These good works were not done to win some annual prize; they did these things from a heart of love to their Heavenly Father and their neighbor. I pray that our family will be as dedicated as they were!

Diligence is also necessary when ruling or leading (Romans 12:8). Leading our children or others must be done consistently. A half-hearted or unsteady effort at raising our children can lead to insecurity or confusion in their lives. Do not keep them wondering about things like this: Are we cleaning the house/the car this week or not? Are we taking care of the lawn this week or not? Are we going to church this week or not? Diligence on display will answer many questions even before they are asked; it will settle many issues of the heart and mind. Your employer will not wonder if you are going to be at work today. Your neighbor will not wonder if you are going to mow your lawn. Your pastor will not wonder if you are still a member of the congregational flock.

A consistent effort in the area of discipline will also bring many rewards and a lot fewer tears for everyone. Back in the days when I had only three children, I began to see that I was getting angry a little too often, and I did not like how it was affecting my children or myself. I was not abusing them, but I knew I needed to get the edge off my tone.

I began researching the Scriptures. I looked at verses about anger, and I also looked at verses about peace; I actually wrote these verses on paper. When my project was over, it was as if the two topics were hanging in a balance. I could clearly see what God had to say about anger and its effects; I could likewise see the effects of peace, which appeared much more enjoyable to everyone. Now it was time for me to make a decision; would I continue to choose anger, or would I choose the better way of peace?

Of course, I chose peace, but things did not change overnight. I talked with Randal and with the kids about my commitment to choose peace, and I knew it could only be done with the help of the Holy Spirit. There were times when I had to apologize for the re-entrance of the angry character, but then I got right back on track.

Why did I tell this story about anger and peace? Why was it not placed in the "peace" chapter? I know the diligence it took to change my course from anger to peace. I not only became more consistent about disciplining myself but also my children. Rather than telling them to do something three to five times then getting angry, I gave them instructions one time and diligently worked on their obedience; then, everyone was at peace.

I see laziness, slothfulness, or even procrastination as enemies of diligence. We have this scriptural admonition:

"Live purposefully and worthily and accurately, not as the unwise and witless, but as wise...making the very most of the time because the days are evil. Therefore do not be vague and thoughtless and foolish, but understanding and firmly grasping what the will of the Lord is."
(Ephesians 5:15-17, AMP)

The wisdom of Proverbs also instructs women about diligence when it praises the virtuous woman, saying that "she watches over the ways of her household, and does not eat the bread of idleness" (Proverbs 31:27). In the busyness of life, are we continuing to watch over our household? Are we honoring our spouse? Are we loving our children? Are the dinners being prepared? Are the bills being paid? Is the house staying clean? Are the children doing well in their studies? Are we choosing paths that take us toward a better future? (Is this too many questions?) These tasks are achieved little by little, like the strokes of an ax to a tall tree.

Diligence – whether in the practice of an instrument, bodily exercise, or the habit of the common – will cause the weeded ground of neglect to become the verdant garden of usefulness. The dullness of the mundane can blossom into the beauty of the monumental as we persevere. We must stay attentive to our efforts; for though they seem small, there will come a time when the many strokes of our brush will produce a masterpiece.

STRENGTHEN YOUR ROOTS

*Choose to be diligent in your daily life and boot laziness out the door.

*Purpose to lessen TV, social media, or gaming time and increase some meaningful activities such as:

-Consistent Bible reading

-Consistent attendance to school, work, church

-Consistent efforts of cleaning, gardening, walking/fitness workouts

*Discipline your children consistently; do not make them guess about your mood and if the rules are going to apply *this* time.

The Fourth Oak – Fun

As the years pass through a family, snapshots of fun make an interesting photo album. In the years before children, enjoyment for a couple can look like a continuation of the activities that brought them together: dinner and a movie on Friday nights, city- or church-league baseball, the occasional concert or major league sports game, friends at the house for dinner and game night, maybe even hiking and time in the great outdoors.

However, as the children arrive, fun's photos may seem to change from color to black-and-white. Babies and small children, in general, need early bedtimes, making late night with friends almost non-existent. Feedings throughout the night leave Mom and Dad a bit sleep-deprived so that even a movie at the house has to be finished the next evening, and great pleasure is gained from just getting some sleep.

No matter our place on this family trek, moments of enjoyment are a breath of fresh air, **making the fourth oak among our nine: Fun.**

A few merry moments for our family have included vacations at the beach. The kids still talk about the morning walks on the beach with Grandpa and Grandma, finding shells and having good conversations. Another family vacation was a family reunion at a campground in West Virginia with family members converging from all over the country. There was swimming, bike riding on trails, s'mores around the campfire, meals together, late-night card games, and even a moment of family prayer.

Holidays can always provide enjoyment. Fourth of July took us to my brother and sister-in-law's home for eating ice cream and watching fireworks from the bed of a truck. Thanksgiving still brings together my dad's family, who we usually only see once a year; my kids love the food and seeing cousins, aunts, and uncles. At any time of the year, my kids may launch into conversation about our annual Christmas Eve family gathering where the enjoyment goes beyond the food being served, the presents being given, and *A Christmas Story* being watched; it also includes lots of laughs and love.

The boys of our family have had weekend hunting trips with Grandpa, learning about hunting and life around the campfire. The girls of the family have enjoyed day trips with Grandma, eating lunch at a tea room and browsing through antique shops. One time, we attended a movie with some friends. Stretching ourselves out across a long row, as the movie progressed, we passed candy and popcorn back and forth, all the while laughing at the antics of the animated story. Sometimes laughter happens at moments as simple as an evening meal, gathered around the dining table; a funny incident shared with everyone makes the laughter go twice as far.

Since our family has always been involved in church, many of our friendships and much of our activities have been with our church family. Small group gatherings in our home have been a common practice, eating together and sharing what is in our hearts and on our minds. As our children have grown, there have been the happy times of summer church camp and fine arts trips; even church services have been anticipated for spiritual and relational good. Being part of a church family is more than singing songs and hearing the sermon; it is about being part of the same family of faith and sharing common values.

Our church has a unique event every couple of months at our on-site park. The vintage "pot-luck gathering in the fellowship hall" has been combined with the modern elements of outdoor baptism and worship. There are food trucks, tailgating, lots of fellowship, and kids tossing the football or playing in the splash pad. Sometimes there is live jazz music, Latin music, or even the songs of Motown. No matter what is happening, there is a sense of enjoyment in our church community, and sounds of laughter and praises to God reach the deep places of our soul and spirit.

This leads me to say that fun moments are also strengthening moments. They seal within us the love we have for others; for in a relaxed moment, we choose to be with those we love and trust. Scripture includes God's plans for His family to participate in annual feasts and events that brought everyone together, inspiring joy and gladness. In the New Testament, members of the earliest church ate and fellowshipped together.

"So continuing daily with one accord in the temple, and breaking bread from house to house, they ate their food with gladness and simplicity of heart, praising God and having favor with all the people."
(Acts 2:46, 47, NKJV)

A family's celebration moments can include birthdays, weddings, anniversaries, graduations, baptisms, and confirmations. Family gatherings will also include funerals, which at first glance appear somber; but usually, as family and friends converse, there are funny tales or merry moments about the one who passed, reminding all of us that life is to be enjoyed.

Randal's family was always a "game" family. At Christmas and on New Year's Day, family members could be found playing cards and watching football games. I have childhood memories of gathering with family for grilled burgers and homemade ice cream while the men played dominoes, the women sat and talked, and all of us kids ran around outside playing hide-and-seek. I remember my dad playing church-league baseball. Attending those games meant cheering on good friends, playing with the other kids at the ballpark playground, and getting eats from the snack bar.

Fun moments do not necessarily have to be expensive moments. An at-home game night with popcorn and cookies is fun. Everyone cheering for their favorite team while watching championship games together, munching on chips and dips, gives much opportunity for camaraderie, and the win makes it all glorious. These days, electronic or digital games add another dimension to fun moments; our kids enjoyed playing together, and even Randal got involved. Now we have a monthly event called Phelps First Friday where there is good food, enjoyable conversation, and of course, lots of laughs. Our guideline is that if you cannot attend this time, there is always next month.

So far, I have spoken about fun that is achieved by our activities, but beyond this, there is an attitude of joy which can fill our homes with laughter – hearty, genuine laughter. If "a merry heart does good like medicine" (Proverbs 17:22), then we should make sure our families are the healthiest in the neighborhood.

On another note, I believe the enemies of fun might exist at both ends of the spectrum. Being too controlling, especially with children, becomes oppressive and even depressing, which seems to open the door for stiffness to be present in a family. But unlimited – sometimes unsupervised – amusement can lead to a lack of structure, which seems to open the door to laziness or inappropriate actions. The proper balance of fun always calls on us to check our hearts (and calendars, too). There have been times when a busy schedule, laced with fun, has exhausted us and our children. Thinking that "some fun is good, so lots of fun must be better" is like eating too much cotton candy at the fair. However, not providing moments of enjoyment for our family can have the wilting effect of a Texas summer; even in the shade, the breeze is hot.

We have the opportunity to fill the photo album of family life with wonderful, meaningful snapshots of fun. When there are many moments of laughter, there will most likely be fewer moments of sadness. Colorful pics of life being enjoyed ought to be part of our memories, so learn to laugh together. It may or may not create a picture-perfect life, but it *can* make a joyful family.

STRENGTHEN YOUR ROOTS

*Choose fun family moments, and make sure everyone gets involved.

*Have fun-loving traditions for your family, maybe at Thanksgiving or Christmas.

*Chronicle a family event by taking photos and posting on social media or printing a small book about it.

*Bake some cookies with your kids or grandkids.

The Fifth Oak – Service

Have you ever volunteered at your local food pantry? Have you ever served in a political candidate's campaign? Maybe you have taught a Sunday school class or tutored kids in an after-school program. Whether we are speaking about the volunteers in a community or the members of a family, the idea of serving others spreads its roots wide and deep. Because of this, **the fifth oak among our nine is Service.**

When we think of the phrase *serving others*, we might picture a waiter at a restaurant, someone serving in the military, or even actual servants who work at someone's home. But modern-day service speaks of helping and caring for others, most often without compensation: volunteering.

I know of a national association whose members volunteer to train one another regarding the software they all use. They meet in small local groups, serve on committees, and even help at their national conference. Many have been helped over the years to better understand the product they have purchased because someone has taken the time to volunteer and share their experiences. They have also formed lasting business relationships and friendships as they have networked together.

My father served in the military, doing his part to protect and defend our nation. I remember my mom volunteering at my elementary school, being "room mother," overseeing the Christmas and Valentine's parties and being part of the parent-teacher association. My parents taught Sunday school classes at our church, sang in the choir, and participated in church leadership. As I got older, I witnessed my parents' involvement in politics, overseeing the local precinct elections and meetings. They were living a life of service right in front of my eyes, and now I find myself doing some of the same things.

Through the years, Randal played his instrument in the church band, helping with the Sunday worship services. We have both helped in the church nurseries and children's ministries. I coordinated our church's girls' clubs program. Throughout all of this, Randal and I brought our children along for the ride.

When there have been bags to stuff at church with Easter or Halloween candy, our kids participated in the stuffing. When there were chairs to set up or tear down, they set up or tore down. When there were balloons to blow up...well, you guessed it. There have been times when everyone in our family was handed a bag, and we walked around the neighborhood picking up trash. Our family has assisted others with packing and/or moving. These things became the normal behavior and the accepted lifestyle of our family; this is what we did.

We have found that serving others creates opportunities for our own self-discipline, reining in the state of selfishness where we are only thinking about ourselves. The fullest example of this was Jesus Christ Himself:

"Let this mind be in you, which was also in Christ Jesus, who, being in the form of God, did not consider it robbery to be equal with God, but made Himself of no reputation, taking the form of a bondservant, and coming in the likeness of men."
(Philippians 2:5-7, NKJV)

We have also found that helping others underscores the value of humanity, whether they are in a worse condition than we are or not. We can help the old and the young, the rich and the poor, a friend or a stranger. In Stephen Covey's *Seven Habits of Highly Effective People*, he said,

"There is intrinsic security that comes from service, from helping other people in a meaningful way. And there are so many ways to serve. Whether or not we belong to a church or service organization or have a job that provides meaningful service opportunities, not a day goes by that we can't at least serve one other human being by making deposits of unconditional love."

Perhaps my words about this have been few compared to other chapters, but this is because little has to be said concerning it. I see it in this way: we all need help in some way at some point in our lives, so let us help one another. Our families will be better, stronger, and more emotionally healthy when we do.

STRENGTHEN YOUR ROOTS

Choose to help others; opportunities are all around us. Here are a few ideas:

*Help at your local church.

*Help at your local school.

*Give food/supplies and/or your time at the local food pantry.

*Give your time at a retirement or convalescent home.

*Drive seniors to their doctors' appointments or their errands.

*Mentor kids or young people through community programs.

*Mentor those in your community marketplace who have fewer years of business experience.

*Donate blood to a local blood bank.

*Keep your community clean through programs for trash pick up and/or beautification projects.

*Volunteer in the offices of your elected officials or in a campaign.

*Rake leaves, pull weeds, or shovel snow for an elderly neighbor.

*Write letters and contribute necessities (and goodies) to those who are abroad in the military or in missionary service.

*Help with church or city festivals or parades.

*Help restore an area after a natural disaster or help the charities who do.

*Volunteer in your community's Meals On Wheels program.

The Sixth Oak – Boundaries

One morning when my older children were young, we were having a devotional moment before we began school. The story we were talking about was Adam and Eve in the Garden of Eden. As you remember, God had told them they could eat from any tree in the garden, but they could not eat the fruit of the tree of the knowledge of good and evil (Genesis 2:15-17). As a point of reference for the kids, I mentioned how their dad and I had told them they could play in the yard but not in the street. When I asked them why they should not play in the street, their response was that the street was bad. I wanted to chuckle but immediately saw a teaching opportunity.

The kids and I began to talk about boundaries and their purposes. *I* knew the street was not bad, but that was *their* perception. They had been told not to play there; they might get hurt by a vehicle or could cause an accident. We talked about the purpose of the street; it was made as a place for cars to drive not as a place for little children to play. We talked about other boundaries, too, like the fences that line our yards, city limits, and state and national boundaries.

Over the years, my husband and I have had opportunities for many other conversations with our children about boundaries, such as driving in the boundaries of the speed limit or sex in the boundaries of marriage. **The sixth oak among our nine is understanding the purpose of Boundaries.**

To lay a foundation, let us look at the actual Genesis reference:

> "Then the Lord God took the man and put him in the garden of Eden to tend and keep it. And the Lord God commanded the man, saying, "Of every tree of the garden you may freely eat; but of the tree of the knowledge of good and evil you shall not eat, for in the day that you eat of it you shall surely die."
> (Genesis 2:15-17, NKJV)

I do not believe that God makes rules without reasons. When the children of Israel were about to go into the Promised Land, Moses went over the ground rules for living there. While many rules can be seen as one reads through the books of Exodus and Leviticus, Deuteronomy seems to carry a slightly different message. Understanding was given to the people that these things were "for their good" so that things would "go well" for them and their children. I believe the Ten Commandments were not dreamed up to put some huge damper on life; God knew that following such guidelines would be helpful to them and their families, just as it still is to us and our families today.

Similarly, when we tell our children not to eat too much candy, we do not do so with intent to keep them from enjoying life; we actually know too much sugar has negative effects like tummy aches, bad teeth, and hyperactivity. Having our children go to bed at a decent hour is not about keeping them from fun; it is about proper rest, which encourages proper growth and health. As parents, we have many other opportunities to teach our children about guidelines and even hard-and-fast rules.

For all of us, personal boundaries give definition to our lives. The boundary of fidelity designates faithfulness in our marriage relationships. The boundary of honesty defines the value of truth in our culture. The boundary of lawfulness supports honoring others. Many other virtues and disciplines act as boundaries for our lives, which enhance our life experiences and also keep us from bad consequences.

In the Christian faith, Jesus taught about the discipline of fasting, or what one might call the boundary of moderation. Randal and I had practiced fasting once a week for years. I remember wanting to teach our children about it, but I did not know how to incorporate fasting into the life of a child. One day as I was cleaning our kitchen, a Scripture verse that I had framed and hung on our wall caught my eye: "And you shall serve the Lord your God, and He shall bless your bread and your water, and I will take sickness away from the midst of you" (Exodus 23:25, NKJV). In a flash, I saw a combination opportunity: fasting with the result of health. We had been experiencing a few more sniffles than I was comfortable with, which made this the perfect answer.

My husband and I chose one day of each week that we called "bread and water day" for our family to participate in the discipline of fasting, with the goal of keeping indulgence – and sugar – in check. Now before you become outraged that children would have to eat only bread and water, let me explain.

First of all, we had a family meeting and explained what we were doing; we set a date to begin. We usually started our day with homemade muffins with plenty of butter but no jam. We would also allow the children to have milk at this meal, but we would all drink water for the rest of the day. Snack times would be varieties of crackers or even popcorn. Lunch might be pan-sautéed tortillas or buttered bread/buns heated under the broiler. Then, in the afternoon I would set out several dozen dinner rolls to rise. Our evening meal would be freshly baked dinner rolls, once again, with plenty of butter. Throughout the day, the children could eat as much as they liked of these designated items. The goal of the day was to accomplish some type of fasting and curtail our sugar intake.

This day of fasting food also included fasting TV, video games, and music. Things were quiet, but what I always saw happen was an increase of interaction with each other: playing with one another, cards, board games, outside playtime. We also saw a positive health increase, rarely a runny nose or cold.

For years, our church has hosted a prayer and fasting event each year during January and has also practiced Lent near Easter. Once again, we made decisions about what we were going to fast as a family, and we also had the kids select something that they were going to fast individually. (They would sometimes say they were going to fast their school work...laughingly, not an option.) We believe the self-control practiced during times of fasting brings a measure of temperance to our lives that forges strength.

As our children grew, Randal and I began to see the need for our children to live within the boundary of respect for each other's possessions, so we developed the guideline of each child asking permission to play with the other child's toy, meaning that a child could not just go into the other's room and take the other's toy or book or possession; they had to ask permission. This saved many a tear from being shed. If a tear was shed about this, it was easy to trace the offense. Even as the kids got older, they still had to ask the others if they could have a piece of the pizza they had purchased or the soft drinks that belonged to them; something purchased for the entire family certainly did not fall under these guidelines, but individual possessions were respected.

Almost as early as our children could carry on a conversation, we developed the courtesy of allowing others to complete their thought without interruption. This was not as stiff as *Robert's Rules of Order* (a classic book on how to run orderly meetings and discussions), but we believed we should all practice the boundary of no interruption, honoring the words and thoughts of one another.

As I have mentioned previously in this book, strife was not tolerated in our home, a practice that I would probably credit to my mother who did not allow my siblings and me to fuss with one another. Our children knew how to live within the boundary of loving others – no fighting, no hurtful words – or there were consequences.

Putting boundaries in place for a family usually relies on the strength of parents and should originate from a desire of keeping the family on a right path, especially the children. Without boundaries, straying from the path becomes like the chapter in *The Hobbit* where the dwarves and Mr. Baggins leave the path of safety in the dark woods and go toward the magical lights of the wood elves and their merry feast. As you know, spiders then came into the plot, and they almost lost their lives. As parents, we must not allow the merriment of a child's sanguine personality to become the argument for what actually leads to foolishness. Scripture tells us that "foolishness is bound in the heart of a child, but the rod of correction shall drive it far from him" (Proverbs 22:15, NKJV). Following the sometimes narrow path of life keeps us from having to partake of the rod of correction, because foolishness seems to come easy. Boundaries may appear to be constricting, maybe even binding, but when followed, a higher and better way of life emerges.

As parents, we need to lovingly and immediately talk with or discipline our children when they have stepped over the line. I remember parents engaging in some kind of time out or tally system before disciplining their children. With time out, young children do not always remember the nature of the offense when the time is completed, even when it is just a few minutes. With the tally system, children seem to quickly acquire points up to the final one, then exhibit amazing self-control. But Proverbs gives other advice:

> "He who spares his rod hates his son, but he who
> loves him disciplines him *promptly*."
> (Proverbs 13:24, NKJV, emphasis added)

Jesus also spoke of boundaries when He contrasted the broad way and the narrow way:

> "Enter by the narrow gate; for wide is the gate, and broad
> is the way that leads to destruction, and there are many who
> go in by it. Because narrow is the gate, and difficult is the
> way, which leads to life, and there are few who find it."
> (Matthew 7:13, 14, NKJV)

As time passed, our kids learned to throw a football or ride a bike in the street. They also learned about curfews and the proper use of money. Understanding the boundaries that make for good living is still high priority in our four walls; we know that boundaries are for our good so things will go well with us.

STRENGTHEN YOUR ROOTS

*Choose some guidelines that are going to determine your life's path (possibly The Ten Commandments, the teachings of the Sermon on the Mount in Matthew 5-7, or the objectives of Romans 12:9-21), then keep them.

*Agree on and participate in some type of fasting for yourself and your family (no sweets for a day, no electronics for a day). Instead of indulging in a movie tonight, help your parent or elderly neighbor.

*Follow the boundaries of courtesy in conversation; allow someone else to finish their sentence or their thought.

*Take a look at the Ten Commandments. Discuss with your family what society would be like if we lived within these boundaries:

-You shall have no other gods before Me.

(A positive interpretation: God is the most important thing/being in my life.)

-You shall not make a carved image and bow down to it.

(A positive interpretation: I worship God in spirit and in truth.)

-You shall not take the Lord's name in vain.

(A positive interpretation: I honor God and His name.)

-Remember the Sabbath day, to keep it holy.

(A positive interpretation: I set aside a day each week to

remember and worship God.)

-Honor your father and your mother.

(A positive interpretation: I find ways to let my parents know they are special and honored.)

-You shall not murder.

(A positive interpretation: I embrace life.)

-You shall not commit adultery.

(A positive interpretation: I honor marriage, and I love my spouse.)

-You shall not steal.

(A positive interpretation: God supplies my needs.)

-You shall not bear false witness against your neighbor.

(A positive interpretation: I embrace truthful interactions with everyone.)

-You shall not covet.

(A positive interpretation: I am grateful for all I have.)

The Seventh Oak – Radiance

Do you remember playing outside on summer evenings as a child? With bare feet and a little bit of nighttime coolness, the hunt was on for fireflies. Their glow came out of the darkness and enticed us to chase them; it was quite the childhood adventure. These days, we seem to be more enthralled with the lights of a stadium or a stage. And what draws us to these? The perception that what happens under these lights will "wow" us or at least give us a moment's satisfaction.

We turn on a light when we enter a room; we turn on a porch light at night, and we turn on a nightlight for a child. The very obvious truth is that light gets rid of the darkness and allows us to see what we are doing. In the same way, the spiritual light that comes from our lives can illuminate us and those around us. When there is a dark moment in our human experience, perhaps a moment when we do not know what to do or where to go, light from a good source can bring encouragement and direction; therefore, **the seventh oak among our nine is Radiance.**

We all know people who can "light up a room" when they enter. What is it about them that draws our attention? Some kind of personal magnetism bestowed by the gods? The fate of beauty? What kind of light am I talking about? The kind that God creates. Scripture tells us that, in the beginning, "God said, 'Let there be light,' and there was light" (Genesis 1:3, NKJV). I believe that when we release the God-kind of light that resides on the inside of us, people are attracted.

Many times our family has been in a restaurant, and someone has come over to us and complimented us; they were amazed at the well-behaved children or the large family unit all together for a meal. This happened often and at varied places, and we tried to understand it. We just knew that wherever we were, we needed to represent our Heavenly Father and His Kingdom. In doing so, I believe that radiance was the effect.

Here are a few scriptures that mention radiance:

"He [the Lord] will make your innocence radiate like the dawn, and the justice of your cause will shine like the noonday sun."
(Psalm 37:6, NLT)

"Those who look to him for help will be radiant with joy; no shadow of shame will darken their faces."
(Psalm 34:5, NLT)

"From Mount Zion, the perfection of beauty, God shines in glorious radiance."
(Psalm 50:2, NLT)

One of the aspects of being radiant is that we are "marked by or expressive of love, confidence, or happiness" (Merriam-Webster's Collegiate Dictionary, Tenth Edition). Most people find such things refreshing in these times of negative messages. When we live in a loving, confident, and happy way, it contrasts the darkness of this world's pessimistic view: one that says we are all going to die from cancer, that we never know when violence will strike next, that every family is dysfunctional, or that we can never be too careful with money. There has to be some shining message in the world, or darkness will swallow us.

God told the prophet Isaiah to declare:

"Arise, shine; for your light has come, and the glory of the
Lord is risen upon you. For behold, the darkness shall cover
the earth, and deep darkness the people; but the Lord shall
arise over you, and his glory will be seen upon you.
And the Gentiles shall come to your light, and kings
to the brightness of your rising."
(Isaiah 60:1-3, NKJV)

We can heed the same message today because darkness is all around us. What kind of darkness am I talking about? The darkness of cynicism, of confusion, of injustice, darkness that steals, kills, destroys, darkness that swaps good for bad, right for wrong, innocence for guilt, darkness that dims the light until we can no longer see life in its true form.

God's directive to the prophet was for the people to arise and shine in the midst of darkness. The action seemed to promise good results: the Lord arising over them, His glory being seen, people coming to the light. So how do we arise and shine? Where do we even begin?

The Bible is our main source of Light, so let us look there.

"Your word is a lamp to my feet and a light to my path."
(Psalm 119:105, NKJV)

"The entrance of Your words gives light; it gives
understanding to the simple."
(Psalm 119:130, NKJV)

When we read the Bible, we are choosing the opportunity to be enlightened about God, about the human experience, about a better way to live. The words of the Bible, God's words, give us understanding about how to live a life that shines. People notice the light of a good marriage; people notice the light of children honoring their parents and grandparents; people notice the light of honesty; people notice the light of generosity. All these ideas produce a radiant lifestyle, and all these ideas are from God and His Word, the Bible.

As my children were growing up, I read the Bible to them every day, not just so they would know the stories of Noah and the ark or David and Goliath, but so they would understand God's ways, themes that were like seeds planted in their hearts and minds. I knew the Scriptures would shape the lives of my children and speak like a voice whether I was present with them or not.

We all need the light that comes from God, so we should start by asking Him to be the Light in our lives. A simple prayer, acknowledging Jesus as the Light of the world – God's answer to darkness – creates a fellowship between us and the Savior that will illumine us and the people around us.

"In him [Jesus] was life, and the life was the light of men."
(John 1:4, NKJV)

"...God is light and in Him is no darkness at all."
(1 John 1:5, NKJV)

"...if we walk in the light as He is in the light, we have fellowship with one another, and the blood of Jesus Christ His Son cleanses us from all sin."
(1 John 1:7, NKJV)

After asking Him to be the light in our lives, we need to let His light shine through us to others; be a lighthouse. Life is full of not-so-good situations that could actually become disastrous. We often have opportunity to shine our light into the lives of others by praying for them or sharing our own story of God's grace. Helping someone steer clear of the rocky cliffs of human experience and guiding them back into the safe haven of right choices is a noble way to live.

Our light also shines when we help others in a compassionate way like giving food to someone who is hungry, clothes to someone who has little to wear, a ride to or from work to someone who does not have a car.

"You are the light of the world. A city that is set on a hill cannot be hidden. Nor do they light a lamp and put it under a basket, but on a lampstand, and it gives light to all who are in the house. Let your light so shine before men, that they may see your good works and glorify your Father in heaven."
(Matthew 5:14-16, NKJV)

Imagine many houses on a street. Imagine the sun going down and darkness settling in. Imagine one house with its lights on. This house would be distinct. Imagine many people in an office. Imagine dark circumstances weighing them down and hopelessness settling in. Imagine one associate that is radiant with God's goodness. This person would be distinct.

Whether we are speaking about the guiding rays of a lighthouse, the warmth of a porch light, or the inner brightness of a human spirit, light illuminates the darkness and draws our attention. Likewise, allowing the radiance of God's light to shine into our hearts then shine out to others will be an attraction that far surpasses the cool, summer nights and firefly-games of childhood.

STRENGTHEN YOUR ROOTS

*Choose to be the one who "lights up the room" because of your positive attitude and smiling face.

*Invite Jesus, the true Light, into your life, then shine that Light into the lives of others with good works.

*Smile more often; your joy will be radiant, and others will notice.

*Look back at the list of service ideas and do one of them; your good works will help someone and glorify your Heavenly Father.

The Eighth Oak – Authenticity

What is the difference between a diamond ring and costume jewelry? Between a strand of pearls and a string of beads? Between a luxury car and an economy vehicle? I believe we can safely say the disparity of these items is their substance: what they are made of. When comparing some items in life, there may seem to be only a small amount of difference; whereas, other items are worlds apart in value.

Throughout history, there have been those who excelled at manufacturing the artificial. Similarly throughout history, there have been those who have excelled at shopping the artificial. We have probably all visited a thrift store at least once in our lives. Those who relish bargains are usually thrilled to scoop up a product that shimmers like a diamond yet is only a fraction of the cost. Those selling the shimmer are usually thrilled, too. But here is what we inevitably find out: you get what you pay for.

I remember buying bargain clothes for my children, only to find them unraveled after the first time washed, or buying bargain toys at Christmas, only to find them broken within the first hour of play. While many are not used to shopping at the best of stores for the wares of life, parsimonious efforts do not usually pay off.

How about people? Surely we have all had friends or acquaintances who appeared genuine; but as time passed, their unreliable nature became evident. For someone or something to be authentic, it must be genuine, verifiable, and true. *Legit* is one of the words in our culture used to declare that something is real or worth one's attention. The validity of who we are in the truest sense makes **Authenticity the eighth oak among our nine.**

Being genuine is much like being truthful as I wrote in an earlier chapter, but it seems to carry a deeper message; it seems to emerge from a deeper place like the difference between a pond and a spring. Both are water, but one comes from a source deep under the surface. Likewise, a refreshing and untainted life has its origination from the truest Source: God.

We all have options for our empowerment, but unlike the battery commercials that assure us their brand is the most reliable, there really is only One who can be an on-going Source of life for us, One who does not flicker, move into the shade, offer compromise, or become inconsistent like the effects of a twist in a hose.

I believe authenticity is like a calling to be lived throughout life, choosing to be the proverbial city set on a hill. What would happen if the source of the spring became tainted? What would happen if the lighthouse no longer shined its light? If the GPS failed to work? If pure gold was mixed with another metal? If the North Star dimmed?

Consistently living in a genuine way produces a reliability that others can trust. I remember a sibling scuffle that happened with a neighbor's children which my children witnessed. When the mom arrived in the backyard trying to get the truth about the situation, she asked my children what happened; she said she knew they always told the truth. The compliment was their reliability. What made them reliable? Their substance of truthfulness, their genuine nature.

What is the Source of this genuine substance I am speaking of? God, His reliably true words of the Bible, and His amazingly sure ways through time. Everything about Him is pure and sound. Having Him as the Source of our substance causes us to be pure and sound, as pure and sound as possible on this side of Heaven. We have the opportunity to walk throughout life as Jesus did, empowered by the life that resides in Heaven, much like the grapes that grow on a vine are the product of being attached to the vine.

Authentic substance is needed in these times of not knowing who to believe. When it comes to media coverage of a story, it is sometimes difficult to know what really happened without wading through the muck of political spin. When I think of a Bible character with no spin, I think of Daniel in the Old Testament. He had lived such a blameless life that when others schemed his downfall, they could find nothing about him that was wrong; he was squeaky clean. We can choose the same substantive path.

If the true way of life is available, why do so many choose the artificial? Scripture speaks of false testimony, false ways, a false tongue and lips, a false balance, a false gift, a false vision and dreams, false prophets, false teachers, false brethren, and even false Christs. Those who do not live from God's ever-reliable life-source finally show their true colors like wearing a cheap ring that tarnishes and turns one's finger that tell-tale green color. Surely the ingredients of falsehood consist of that which is sub-grade, shallow, and even decaying so that it dries up and is blown away by the wind. The bottom line is this: "Keep yourself far from a false matter…" (Exodus 23:7, NKJV).

Galatians 5 speaks about evidence of a natural life and fruit of a Spirit-filled life. The natural life is selfish and produces a list of unattractive characteristics: adultery, fornication, uncleanness, lewdness, idolatry, sorcery, hatred, contentions, jealousies, outbursts of wrath, selfish ambitions, dissensions, heresies, envy, murders, drunkenness, and revelries. If any of these things are making an appearance in our life, we need to re-think some things. On the contrary, the Spirit-filled life has a much better showing: love, joy, peace, patience, kindness, goodness, faithfulness, gentleness, and self-control. When these qualities appear, we can be sure we are connected to the True Vine, the real Source of a genuine life.

Here is my conclusion and hopefully my testimony. We dare not parade our ring as a diamond when it is only of the crystal variety. We dare not live our lives like the tricks of a magician whose razzle-dazzle is only a front for illusion. We dare not make pretenses of genuineness, for there always seems to be a moment of reckoning when the truth is told. In that moment, our substance must exceed the base standard of the artificial and excel to true gold. While many things in life look real, let us as individuals and families be the examples of authenticity, as pure and deep as a spring of water.

STRENGTHEN YOUR ROOTS

*Choose authenticity for yourself and your family so that others know you are genuine.

*Be the reliable associate in your office or student in your class.

*Take a second glance at your reading sources, at your news sources, at your friends. Are they truthful? If not, make a switch.

*Ask yourself about the "fruit' coming from your life. Does the list look like the natural life or the Spirit-filled life?

The Ninth Oak – Creativity

Imagine singers or musicians performing a song; architects designing a new building; townspeople planting flowers in a neighborhood park; preschoolers gluing macaroni onto a Mother's Day card. To place the very words on this page, to brush color on a canvas, to portray a character in a play, all of this flows from the creative genius inside us, like some stream or river that gurgles with beauty. That is how I see **our ninth oak: Creativity.**

Creativity seems to push the boundaries past mental limits. About the time one thinks "I have seen everything," some new design will pop up and surprise. Even the refresh of an old design makes us tend to wonder, "Why didn't we think of that the last time that was in style?" Walk through a museum or just a school art exhibit and you see ideas that have made it past the limits of inside-thinking to outside-showing for all to see. Listen to any kind of music, and one is amazed at what musicianship offers – from thrills to blue moods.

I have long been amazed at the talents of our family members: painting, interior design, graphic design, cabinetry, fashion, music, horticulture, cooking. But why should creativity amaze? We are made in the image of the Creator of the Universe. I believe we are *all* creative, but what will we do with such ability? As we are inspired, let us create. Imagine, draw, paint, sew, plant, build, hum, sing, strum, strike out the rhythm, tap the beat, spin, write the words, form the sentences. It is all there, waiting for us to give it form, waiting for us to enjoy, waiting for us to pass it on and amaze others.

Creativity also seems to walk hand-in-hand with resourcefulness. Have you ever been around someone who could re-decorate a room with just a couple of changes, and yet there was a whole new look? Have you ever looked in your freezer or pantry, thinking you had nothing, and come up with a week's worth of meals? Refreshed an old outfit with some great shoes, a denim jacket, or a vintage brooch?

One time, our family purchased and updated an older home as an investment project; the house had been sitting empty for several years when we bought it. We had the floors leveled, we painted inside and out, we had new carpet installed, we planted flowers and shrubs, and we thoroughly cleaned it. When it sold, it looked like a different place.

My youngest daughter once was invited to a neighbor's home for a birthday party; it was spur-of-the-moment with no time to get to the store and purchase a gift. She made a "rose" pen, then she found a glow wand she had received at church kid's camp. She put it all in a gift bag, added a cute card on which she wrote the name in a creative way, and the little girl loved it. The family was also celebrating a boy cousin's birthday at the same party, so we had our son assemble a couple of Lego cars with an accompanying ramp for the boy's gift. Big hit!

Another time, I was given a very large case of applesauce. I knew we could not eat all of it, so I found a recipe in a cookbook my grandmother had given me for applesauce coffeecake (recipe in the back of the book). I made several coffeecakes, wrote notes of encouragement, and gave them to friends and neighbors. The applesauce was used wisely, and the friends were encouraged. There have been times I cut a rose from our rose bush, put it in a vase, and took it to a friend as a hostess gift when we had been invited to dinner. As our children have outgrown their clothes, I washed them, made sure they were in good shape, and gave them to someone else. Creativity can flourish through our resources while we are also blessing and encouraging others.

But what if we have little in our hand with which to be resourceful? Situations with little resource open the door to miraculous happenings. Think of the stories in the Bible: the earth was "without form and void," and God spoke words that caused it to change (Genesis 1:1, 2). Elisha of the Old Testament blessed a small amount of food that ended up feeding many with some left over (2 Kinds 4:42-44). This same thing happened in the New Testament when Jesus fed thousands with just a few fish and loaves of bread (Matthew 15:32-38, Mark 8:1-9).

Paul of the New Testament spoke about a group that had very little but ended up being a big blessing to others:

"Moreover, brethren, we make known to you the grace of God bestowed on the churches of Macedonia, that in a great trial of affliction the abundance of their joy and their deep poverty abounded to the riches of their liberality."
(2 Corinthians 8:1, 2, NKJV)

What happened? When they decided to open up their hearts and share joyfully with others, God empowered the things they gave so that altogether their giving ended up being abundant and helped many. Likewise, let us not despise the little amount we may think we possess; give with joy and see how far it goes. Let us not wait until we have "the big house" before we invite someone to join us for dinner. I remember Randal and me inviting family or friends to our one-bedroom apartment for a meal. Let us not wait until we can give $1,000 to charity or in the church offering; start with $1, $5, $10, or $25. There have been times when I scooped the change out of my wallet to give at church or to a charity during the holidays. When we do these things joyfully, the creation that emerges will be startlingly enjoyable and will also bless others.

When we deal with situations that seem to have little substance, we can speak faith-filled, creative words to bring about change the same way our Creator did when He created the world and humanity. When our finances are low, we can speak words of abundance such as, "He supplies all our need according to His riches in glory" (Philippians 4:19, NKJV), then keep believing for things to turn around. Over the years, we have been blessed by God's goodness as we said similar things, and He opened doors for extra jobs for Randal or me to work. Or someone at church walked up and said God had impressed upon them to give us some money. Or we received a check in the mail, maybe the return of a deposit on a utility account, which was perfect timing. Faith that God is our Provider rose up in our spirit, filled our words, and *created* sufficiency, fullness, and even abundance.

In moments of sickness, we have spoken words of healing and health to ourselves and our children and seen fever go away, swelling go down, viruses end in a couple of days when it was lasting a couple of weeks with others. We often said things like, "We are healed with the stripes of Jesus" (Isaiah 53:5; 2 Peter 2:24, NKJV). Faith that God is our Healer rose up in our spirit, filled our words, and *created* health.

The Bible is full of God's promises. When we speak them out loud, we are reminded of God's answers for our lives. We create something with new form. We shape a new mentality for ourselves. We expand the limits beyond the norm. When our children were young and we still helped them dress, we would have them say a few confessions from the Bible, such as:

*Like Jesus, I grow in wisdom and stature; I become strong in spirit. I am filled with wisdom, and the grace of God is on me. I increase in favor with God and man. (Luke 2:40, 52)
*I obey my parents, for this is right. I honor my father and mother which is the first commandment with promise, that things may go well for me, that I may live long on the earth. (Ephesians 6:1)
*Like Samuel, I grow, and the Lord is with me. He does not let any of my words fall to the ground. (1 Samuel 3:19)
*I am mighty on the earth. (Psalm 112:3)
*Great is my peace, for I am taught of the Lord. (from Isaiah 54:13)

The truest miracle is that God can make a new creation out of *us,* a person, a couple, a family (2 Corinthians 5:17; Galatians 6:15). If God is not part of your life, you may not have the perception that you are in need of any kind of new renovation, but imagine a completely new look for your life. Asking Jesus to be the Savior and Lord of your life takes you from darkness to light, from being an outsider to being a member of God's family, from hopeless to hopeful. (See the back of this book for a Prayer of Salvation.)

Perhaps an enemy of creativity is fear of change. If you are someone who does not like things to change, you probably will not embrace your spouse's rearranging the furniture or buying new furniture. You might not be open to new color on the walls or new spices in your meals. But being open to the creative flow of your spouse or family member – within reason – can be as refreshing as opening the windows of your home when the spring or fall breezes begin to blow.

If you are someone creative, be sure to keep the flow in its boundaries. Rearranging the furniture *every* week might have your toe finding it in the middle of the night when the lights are off...ouch! One of my children always loved to do crafts, but she did not always know what to do with them when she was finished; it was just the doing of the craft that she found so fun. (Confidentially, I do not believe there would be a house or museum big enough to display all her pictures and projects.)

The general rule of our home when the kids were young was that the picture or creation got to be on the refrigerator for one week, then it came down. During that week, we gave lots of compliments; but after that week, it either went into a folder of artwork or into the trash. This may not sound like a mom who was encouraging the blossoming of her children's creative genius, but with seven kids, there would have been no empty space left on *any* wall. What I found was that after a week, the children were not really excited about it anymore; when asked what *they* wanted to do with it, they usually said to throw it away. We kept a few things that have been fun to look at – always a precious moment.

When everyone was finished schooling, I undertook a large project to sort through the years of school work; I had kept all of it. I went through each school year for each child and kept a few things for them and a few for me. Then, at a family gathering, I gave them to everyone; it was almost like Christmas. There were lots of oohs and ahhs and reminiscing.

Some people believe substances can enhance our creativity, substances such as drugs or alcohol; however, my encouragement is to lean toward the Creator of the Universe rather than substances for inspiration.

On a different note, creativity generally seems to have a life-giving aura about it; think of a newborn baby. When it specifically comes to the creation of a child, I encourage husbands and wives to embrace life, even if it is not planned. In our own story, one of our children was quite the surprise. Unfortunately, I allowed some dark days to trouble me because the pregnancy was not part of *my* plan; but like most surprises that come into our lives, this child brought much happiness and is a treasure. Almost from the moment of birth, new joy filled my heart that began to replace the sadness I had allowed to simmer there. While I always encourage husbands and wives to be in agreement about having children or *not* having children, our story is a beautiful testimony to the fact that God has purpose for a created life, even if we find ourselves at a place of surprise.

Allowing creativity to flourish in your family and home is like painting fresh color on God's design for us or writing a new verse for the song of our lives. In our personal story or the one we are writing for our family, let us dare to be creative; let us dare to be a new creation. Imagine that!

STRENGTHEN YOUR ROOTS

*Choose to let creativity be present in your family by encouraging creative moments.

*Go to a new restaurant this Friday night and celebrate your accomplishments for the week.

*Choose a new vacation destination.

*Color in a coloring book or add some color to your journal entries.

*Add some color to your home with a piece of furniture, pillows, or curtains, or paint new color on some walls in the house.

*Come to a place of agreement with your spouse about rearranging the furniture.

*Write and publish a song. Write and publish a book.

*Try a new recipe or add some new ingredients to an old one.

*Make sure your life has been newly created by asking Jesus to be your Savior and Lord.

The Forest – Legacy

If you "can't see the forest for the trees," then by all means, rent a helicopter and do a flyover. Certainly what I mean by this silly saying is: **change your perspective**. The beauty of something as grand as a forest cannot eclipse the value of a solitary tree, and yet one solitary tree is not a forest. The only reason a forest exists is because of the trees. Likewise, the greatness of a family is enhanced by the personality, the talents, and the contribution of each of its members, making it a thing of beauty to behold.

As I conclude this book's story of our family, I want to cover the theme of legacy. I see it as the picture of single, standing trees that have grown into a forest, the reality of individuals with unique talents and abilities who have become a family with common destiny and purpose.

Sometimes when we speak of legacy, our thoughts take us toward the future, to our children; this is certainly true. But I believe we must also look at those who blazed the trail before we even had a name: our grandparents, our great-grandparents. What kind of life did they reach for? What dreams did they embrace? For some, it was immigrating to a nation of freedom and prosperity. For some, it was being the first to go to college.

For some, it was starting a business. For some, it was reaching for higher spiritual, philosophical, or political goals.

My paternal grandparents were hard-working people who decided to start their own business. They purchased land on the edge of a town and created the setting for a mobile home community; my grandfather even dug the well for the water. We saw them live the art of dealing with humanity in its many forms from the well-paying customer to the occasional charity case. Their entrepreneurial spirit affected all of us in the family, and several grew up to create their own businesses.

What I most remember about my maternal grandparents was their hospitality and kindness. As soon as we walked into their home and had received an ample amount of hugs, we were asked if we would like some kind of refreshments. Many an Easter Sunday saw the whole family gathered for Nana'rie's (Nana Marie) ham and its accompanying spread, then we had the fun of an Easter egg hunt. We were constantly offered roasted pecans by my grandfather, and we even ate his green ice cream when they would host a Chinese-food night.

Interestingly, both couples had previous marriages that had ended in divorce, but they made diligent efforts to keep this second commitment alive, and they supported the institution of marriage. We all gleaned from their strength of character.

So now that *we* have an opportunity to pass something along to our children, what will it be? Beyond any kind of monetary inheritance, what *spiritual* inheritance will we leave to our children? What is it that we want our children to embrace? What are the values we find so life-giving that we cannot breathe without them? From what have we or our ancestors broken free? To what must we anchor ourselves so that we never drift back there? Have we articulated these things to our children?

Legacy is God's idea. In the Old Testament, God often said that His people were to "teach these commands to your children and your children's children..." (Deuteronomy 4:9, NKJV). Today, we are still God's family, and we still have the mandate to observe the principle of legacy. The Light must continue, or the world will become a dark place. The Salt must continue, or the world will have no flavor. Our families must be able to give Living Water and the Bread of Life to those who are spiritually thirsty and hungry.

Perhaps you are at a moment when your family is just beginning. Believe for its life. Contend for its life. Sometimes this has to be done literally. You may have been given a doctor's report that the life in your womb looks as if it will not continue. Contend for it! Speak *life* to that precious life.

With several of my pregnancies, I dealt with pre-term labor; and with each pregnancy, it started earlier. My first child was born four weeks early; my second child was born six weeks early. With my third child, there was daily monitoring and medication, several trips to the hospital, and my eighth month was spent in bed. However, by my fourth pregnancy, there were several scriptures that I found and confessed (I said them out loud) which began to turn the situation around. This **changed my perspective,** and pre-term labor never had the same power again.

Here are the confessions I used based on several verses:

*Like Rebekah and Mary, I deliver my child(ren) when my days are fulfilled and accomplished.
(Genesis 25:24; Luke 2:6)

*I praise God that the life within me is fearfully and wonderfully made. (Psalm 139:14)
*I believe the Lord's report that my baby and I are healed with the stripes of Jesus. (Isaiah 53:1, 5; 1 Peter 2:24)
*God sent His Word and healed me. (Psalm 107:20)

I must truthfully say that we never faced a life-threatening situation with our children after they were born, but we did face spiritual issues that required us once again to contend for the life we believed we and our children should be living.

As we know, the actual birthing process requires strength. As Christian parents, we are most likely called upon again to "birth" the Christian life for our children. In Galatians, Paul said, "...I travail in birth again until Christ be formed in you" (Galatians 4:19, NKJV), speaking of the church in Galatia. As our children grow, we are hopefully teaching them about God's Kingdom through the example of a godly life and the Scriptures, but there will come a point when they have to embrace this Christian life for themselves; this is where we as parents will most likely have to "travail in birth again until Christ is formed" in them.

This will not be accomplished through nagging and worry, which is the broad and easy path to walk, but rather a narrow place of prayer (sometimes strong prayer) and faith that our Heavenly Father will reveal Himself to them, that they will accept Jesus Christ as their Savior and Lord, and that they will accept the Holy Spirit's guidance for their lives. As parents, if all we can do is fear that our children will make wrong decisions and not embrace a godly life, then there is no joy in having children. **Change your perspective** about the value of their destiny, and contend for your legacy.

Years ago, I had a type of vision, a spiritual picture seen in my mind. Atop a mountain were two standards flying in the wind. One said Peace, and one said Truth. I knew immediately this signified my husband and me, even the meanings of our names. Looking up at the flags were mask-type faces; some were joyful, some were confused, and some were even angry. Nothing really happened beyond this simple picture, but there have been moments since then when people looked at us and our lives in a similar way. In these moments, I felt the same strength of that mountain and the same resoluteness of those flying flags.

This leads me to encourage all of us to be resolute about having a healthy family: spirit, soul, and body. Absolutely stand against manipulative behavior, whether from within your immediate family or from in-laws and extended family. You and your spouse must be in agreement about what is right for your family, including how you raise your children, how you create traditions, or even how you participate in family gatherings. Constantly responding to the pull of society, family, and friends only creates an atmosphere of frustration or the feeling of insanity; it will also give opportunities for deep wounds.

If insanity and deep wounds are what you have experienced, **change your perspective** and begin to take control of your family life again. Set new boundaries so that you can get a clear picture and understanding of what you want for your family. Communicate with one another about what is important, what is valuable. Decide what it will take to get you and yours headed toward the wholeness you desire, then start working on your plan. This is similar to a family realizing their finances are out of control, so they map out a plan to cut extra spending and make some extra income. Even if they are not able to save much at the moment, the fact that they are cutting costs and reducing debts will take them in the right direction. The fact that you are cutting extra activities and reducing pressure from others will take your family in the right direction – the direction of health and wholeness.

If your perception of your family is becoming confused, **change your perspective** like the helicopter ride I mentioned at the beginning of the chapter. Know that the beauty of your family becomes evident when each member is living his/her particular calling, gift, and ability. If there happens to be a fire in your forest, you will have to contend for a healthy atmosphere. But do not worry; think of the fresh, new growth that comes after an area has been burned. God can always bring restoration. If you do not have a fire in your forest, then cultivate it; help it to keep growing and enjoy its beauty.

The introduction of this book mentioned that oaks are known for their strength, and families can also be known for theirs. Like a forest of oaks, the most beautiful families will be obvious because they are living in a right way, in righteousness. And the conclusion of the story about this house with nine oaks is that, as long as God is the Source of its righteousness and strength, He will be the One who gets the glory.

"…in their righteousness, they will be like great oaks
that the Lord has planted for His own glory."
(Isaiah 61:3, NLT)

Thinking Family

Fairy tales and storybook endings are enjoyable to read, but if we have experienced family trauma, dysfunction, or even drama, we may think there is no hope for a healthy family. Many times, it seems that humanity complicates family life beyond what is salvageable. What can be done?

Scripture tells us to renew our mind; this is true for all areas of life.

"...that you put off, concerning your former conduct, the old man which grows corrupt according to the deceitful lusts, and **be renewed in the spirit of your mind**, and that you put on the new man which was created according to God, in true righteousness and holiness."
(Ephesians 4:22-24, emphasis added, NKJV)

"...do not be conformed to this world, but **be transformed by the renewing of your mind**, that you may prove what is that good and acceptable and perfect will of God."
(Romans 12:2, emphasis added, NKJV)

"For the weapons of our warfare are not carnal but mighty in God for pulling down strongholds, casting down arguments and every high thing that exalts itself against the knowledge of God, **bringing every thought into captivity to the obedience of Christ**..."
(2 Corinthians 10:4, 5, emphasis added, NKJV)

Scripture and science agree regarding the hope of renewing paradigms and rewiring thought patterns. Begin to see a picture of what a healthy family would look like. What would some action steps be? It is always best to begin with ourselves. How do *my* actions and attitudes help create a positive atmosphere in our home? How do *my* actions and attitudes generate a negative atmosphere in our home?

Positive attitudes in the home are energizing to the soul. A simple smile on our face encourages a spouse or a child. Laughter strengthens the roots of a family tree. When my husband and I have had a hug or peck on the lips, the children always responded; even our dog has sometimes responded.

Negative attitudes in the home are draining to the soul. Even young children are aware of drama between parents; they are aware of dysfunction when it is being openly discussed or yelled through a bedroom door, and it wearies them. They are capable of feeling the angst, even if they might not be able to articulate it. Sometimes it shows itself through crying or through quietness. Dysfunctional scenarios create opportunities for fear and uncertainty, which makes a child wonder about the stability of his/her world.

First of all, choose hope over cynicism. The fortress of family should not be smashed like a tower of blocks just because we personally had a bad experience with father, mother, siblings, or extended family members; the same is true for interactions with in-laws. Human history has shown the good as well as the bad, so a healthy family is possible.

"...with God all things are possible."
(Matthew 19:26; Mark 10:27, NKJV)

Second, choose to believe there is an answer for every situation and know that it might take some time to discover the answer(s).

"...all things are possible for him who believes."
(Mark 9:23, NKJV)

Third, choose forgiveness. We must forgive ourselves and others to make progress and move forward. Additionally, I have personally found that praying for the one(s) I am forgiving speeds the healing process. Forgiveness, much like love, has an action element (verb); it is not just an ethereal, vaporous idea (noun) that makes us feel good in our heart. We must release and disentangle from the dysfunction of our past and from unhealthy interactions with others.

"And be kind to one another, tenderhearted, forgiving one another, even as God in Christ forgave you."
(Ephesians 4:32, NKJV)

Fourth, choose prayer. When a negative lifestyle has become the all-too-familiar lifestyle in our home, pray. Ask the Lord for help and answers, then believe for His help and answers.

"The effective, fervent prayer of a
righteous man avails much."
(James 5:16, NKJV)

To avoid cognitive dissonance, our words need to align with our thoughts and actions. Here are some scriptural confessions for family:

Husbands
*I love my wife as Christ loves the Church and as I love myself. (Ephesians 5:25-33)
*I am not bitter towards my wife. (Colossians 3:19)
*I honor my wife. (1 Peter 3:7)
*I treat my wife as an equal partner of God's grace so my prayers are not hindered. (1 Peter 3:7)

Wives
*I am subject to my husband as the Church is to Christ. (Ephesians 5:21-24)
*I respect my husband. (Ephesians 5:33)
*I love my husband. (1 Corinthians 13)

Fathers
*Like the Lord, I am a compassionate father. (Psalm 103:13)
*I have godly and wise children. (Proverbs 23:24)
*I lovingly correct my children. (Proverbs 3:12)
*As an example to my children, I honor *my* father and mother. (Exodus, 20:12; Ephesians 6:2)
*I do not aggravate or provoke my children. (Ephesians 6:4; Colossians 3:21)

Mothers

*As an example to my children, I honor *my* father and mother. (Exodus, 20:12; Ephesians 6:2)
*When I instruct my children, I do it with kindness. (Proverbs 31:26)
*I get up early and prepare breakfast for my family. (Proverbs 31:15)
*I make sure my children are clothed properly. (Proverbs 31:21)
*I teach the Scriptures to my children. (Deuteronomy 6:7; 2 Timothy 3:15)

Children

*I obey and honor my parents. (Ephesians 6:1-3)
*I pay attention to my parents' correction. (Proverbs 4:1)
*As a child, I am humble, but I am great in God's Kingdom. (Matthew 18:4)
*As I grow up, I put away childish things. (1 Corinthians 13:11)

Once again, here are some action steps to achieve health in our families:

1) Choose hope.
2) Choose to believe for answers.
3) Choose forgiveness.
4) Choose prayer.

Let us renew our mind about our family experience. Thinking about family can bring joy and peace rather than sorrow and anger. Thinking about family can cause us to grow like a healthy plant rather than wilt like a dying flower. Thinking about family gives opportunity for positive rather than negative energy. Thinking about family can take us toward promise and truth rather than instability and lies. Renewal and transformation are the children of reborn thoughts, and what a lovely family *that* is!

The Back of the Book

Prayer for Salvation

Heavenly Father, I confess that I am a sinner. I accept Jesus as my Savior, and I thank You for His sacrifice on the Cross. I want Jesus to be the Lord of my life, helping me every day with strength and wisdom. I accept the Bible as God's Word and His direction for my life. When I pass from this life, I know I will spend eternity in Heaven. Amen.

Recipe for Applesauce Coffeecake
Ingredients:
*1 ½ cups flour, divided into two ¾ cup amounts
*1/2 cup brown sugar
*1 stick salted butter (1/2 cup), cold and cut into chunks
*1/3 cup pecans, chopped (more, if desired)
*1 tsp. cinnamon, divided into ½ tsp. amounts
*1 ½ tsp. baking powder
*1/2 tsp. baking soda
*2 eggs, beaten
*1 cup applesauce (use cinnamon applesauce, if desired)
*1 tsp. vanilla

Instructions:

Preheat oven to 375 degrees. Spray 9x9 baking dish with non-stick cooking spray.

In a bowl, combine butter with brown sugar and ¾ cup of the flour, using a pastry blender until it becomes crumbly.

Topping: Remove ½ cup of mixture and place it in a small bowl. Add to this, the chopped pecans and ½ teaspoon of cinnamon. Mix to combine. Set aside.

Add to the remaining mixture, baking soda, baking powder, eggs, vanilla, applesauce, and the rest of the flour and cinnamon. Beat until smooth.

Pour into prepared dish and sprinkle with topping.

Bake for 30-35 minutes or until toothpick inserted in center of the cake comes out clean.
Serve warm. *Bon appétit!*

About the Author

Angela Phelps resides in Texas with her husband Randal and their Miniature Schnauzer, Paisley. They have raised their family in the North Texas area and home educated their seven children. The children are all grown now, with several of them beginning to raise their own families. She loves being near her children and grandchildren as well as extended family. She enjoys teaching, reading, traveling, and early morning walks.

When not teaching or writing, she studies neuroplasticity, brain health, and renewal of the mind. Based on the scripture in 2 Timothy 1:7, she leads small groups with the purpose of encouraging positive mental health.

She is currently developing several other book projects, including books for children.

Acknowledgments

*"To the Father of Our Lord Jesus Christ, from whom
the whole family in heaven and earth
is named..."
(Eph. 3:14, NKJV)*

*To Randal for your constant encouragement
throughout our journey*

To Alexander for your optimism and creativity

To Krista for your expertise and patience

Follow Angela on Instagram at:
@NineOaksBook

If you enjoyed reading, please leave a positive review for
The House with Nine Oaks on Amazon and Goodreads.

Made in the USA
Monee, IL
02 June 2023

34994719R00056